The WORLD'S GREATEST SOUTHERN GOSPEL SONGS

50
Southern Gospel Classics

COMPILED BY JUDY SPENCER NELON AND NILES BOROP.

Shawnee Press

EXCLUSIVELY DISTRIBUTED BY

HAL•LEONARD®
CORPORATION

7777 W. BLUEMOUND RD. P.O. BOX 13819 MILWAUKEE, WI 53213

SB1015

FOREWORD

This book was made possible through an amazing group of talented folks with strong opinions on which 50 songs qualify for this collection. Over and over, the same songs and composers showed up on each list: Bill and Gloria Gaither, Mosie Lister, Ira Stanphill, Stuart Hamblen, Doris Akers and Squire Parson along with other composers' songs were requested. These names and their hundreds of songs would make a best-selling songbook any day.

How Great Thou Art and *He Touched Me*, two of the greatest songs in gospel music are heard not only at southern gospel concerts but at almost any church or concert genre as well. What makes a great song is that it can be performed by most singers in any genre of music. In the publishing world there is a saying: "When a good singer sings a good song, it is a good song. When a bad singer can sing a good song, it is still a good song. When a bad singer sings a bad song, it is really a bad song. And when a good singer sings a bad song, it is still a bad song." Well, the songs in this book have been proven again and again to be worthy of most any voice or instrument. You have heard these favorite songs over the years. Now here in one collection, these 50 songs are for everyone to enjoy.

We hear about "career songs" and there are those in this collection. Many artists continue to search for their "career song." Even with the best voice, without the right song the world might never hear that singer. There are new artists who start with known standard songs, as the recording companies realize buyers of music seem to appreciate hearing songs they already know. Sometimes popular singers have challenges introducing a new song. New songs must be well written to stand the test against the standards already loved and appreciated.

According to sales reports, Elvis Presley is the world's most popular singer. Elvis grew up in Memphis, regularly attending church and listening to southern gospel music, which made a significant impact on his style. After his concerts, he often invited the back-up singers on his tours to sing with him for hours his favorite gospel songs (not the new ones, but the ones he had always known). One could therefore say southern gospel songs influenced the music heard around the world.

Much appreciation goes to those that contributed to the success of this book and especially Mark Cabaniss and Wayne Yankie, and all the team at Shawnee Press. Their support and enthusiasm for these songs made this a great pleasure!

-Judy Spencer Nelon

We Shall Behold Him

Words and Music by
Dottie Rambo

4

How Great Thou Art

Stuart K. Hine

Swedish Folk melody
Adapted by Stuart K. Hine

Because He Lives

William J. and Gloria Gaither

William J. Gaither

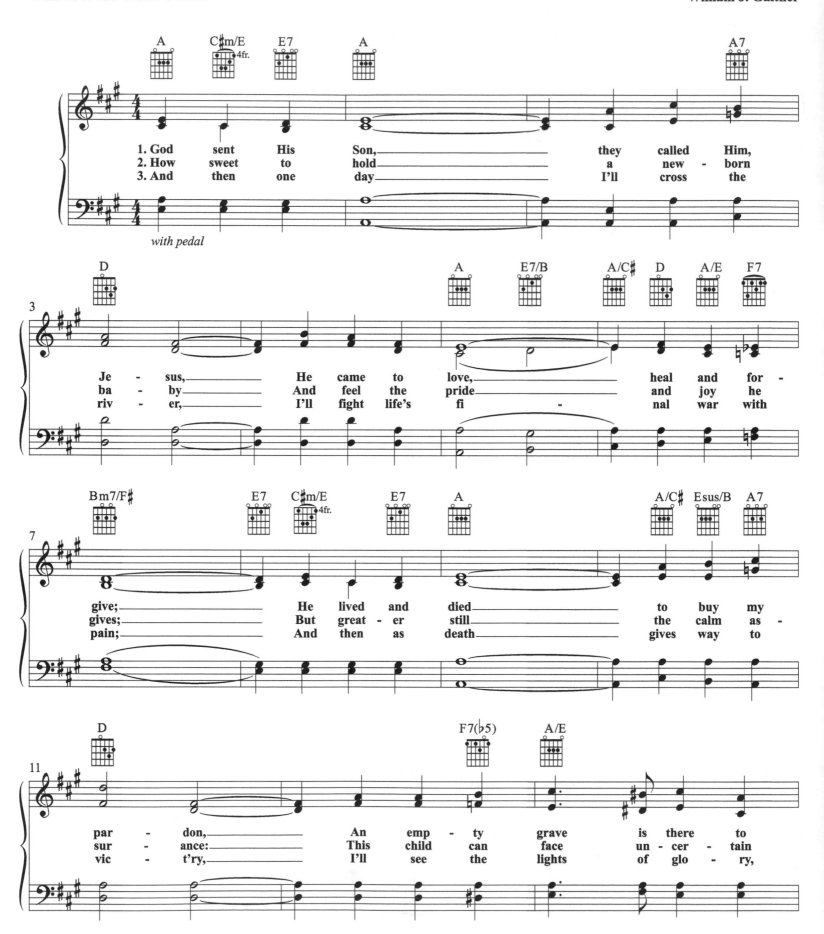

Sweet, Sweet Spirit

Words and Music by
Doris Akers

1. There's a sweet, sweet Spir - it in this place, And I
2. There are bless - ings you can - not re - ceive 'Til you
3. If you say He saved you from your sin, Not you're

know that it's the Spir - it of the Lord; There are
know Him in His full - ness and be - lieve; You're the
weak, you're bound and can - not en - ter in; You can

sweet ex - pres - sions on each face, And I
one to prof - it when each you say, "I am
make it right if when you will yield, You'll en -

know they feel the pres - ence of the Lord.
going to walk with Je - sus all the way."
joy the Ho - ly Spir - it that we feel.

He Touched Me

Words and Music by
William J. Gaither

Daystar
(Shine Down on Me)

Words and Music by
Steve Richardson

1. __ Li - ly of the Val - ley,__ let Your sweet a - ro - ma fill my life, Rose of Shar - on, show me__ how to grow in beau - ty in God's sight; feat. __ Then I Fair - est of Ten thou - sand,__

2. I see a world that's dy - ing,__ wound - ed by the mas - ter of de - ceit; Grop - ing in the dark - ness,__ haunt - ed by the years of past de - see You stand - ing near me,__

Grace
with "Grace Greater than Our Sin"

Words and Music by
Pamela Furr, Raymond Davis and Wayne Haun

D.S. al Fine

I Know Who Holds Tomorrow

Words and Music by
Ira F. Stanphill

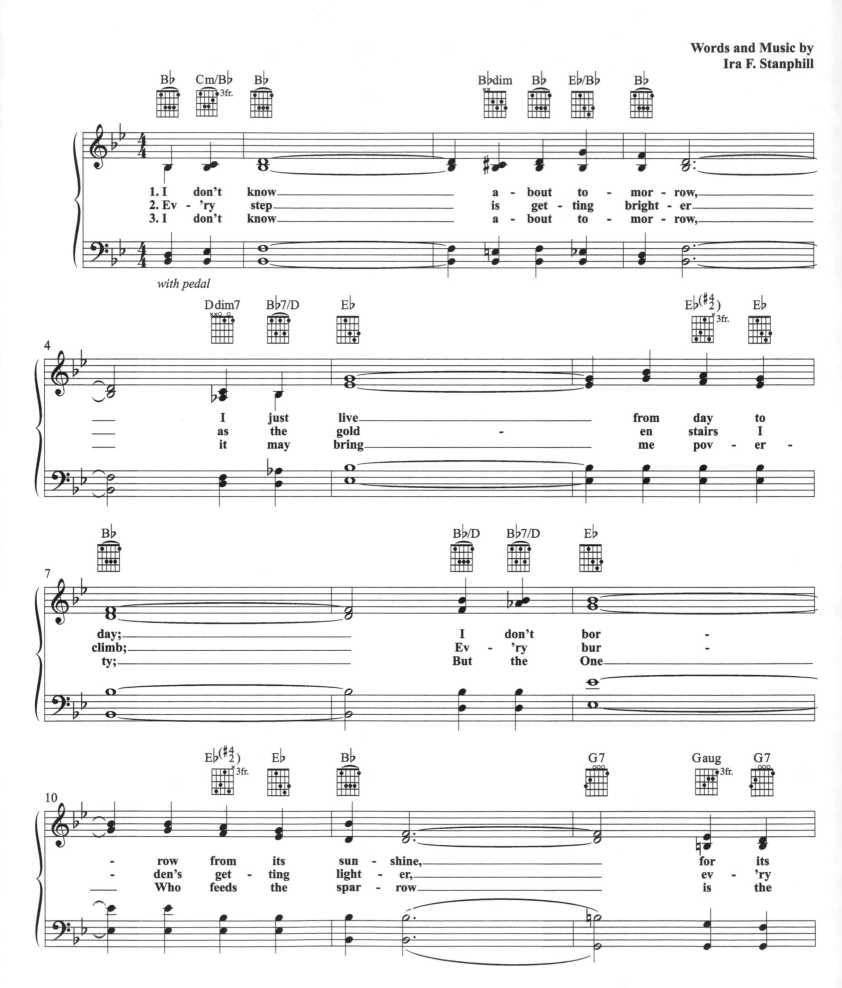

Thank You, Lord, for Your Blessings

Words and Music by
The Easter Brothers

There's Something About That Name

William J. and Gloria Gaither

William J. Gaither

Get Away, Jordan

Traditional Spiritual

Get a - way,— get a - way!

Cues: Instrument or Voice

Get a - way, get a - way,_____ Toom, toom, toom, toom,

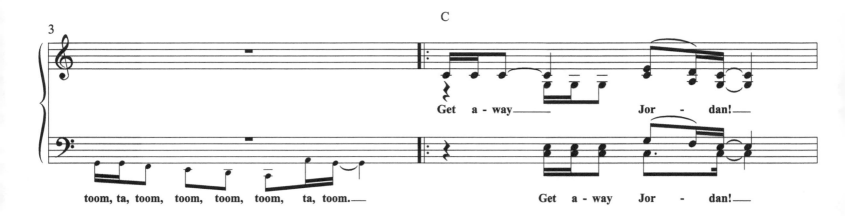

Get a - way_____ Jor - dan!_____

toom, ta, toom, toom, toom, toom, ta, toom._____ Get a - way Jor - dan!_____

F/C C7 F/C C

Get a - way,_____ Well, oh,_____ get a - way, oh, chil - ly Jor-dan! I

get a - way old chil - ly Jor-dan, Get a - way, Jor - dan, I

1.

F C

want to cross o - ver Well, oh,_____

want to cross o - ver to see my Lord._____

2.

F C

want to cross o - ver Well,_____ 1. I

want to cross o - ver to see my Lord._____

Goodbye, World, Goodbye

Words and Music by
Mosie Lister

Midnight Cry

Words and Music by
Greg Day and Chuck Day

If We Never Meet Again

Words and Music by
Albert E. Brumley

I'll Fly Away

Words and Music by
Albert E. Brumley

Sweet Beulah Land

**Words and Music by
Squire Parsons, Jr.**

Until Then

Words and Music by
Stuart Hamblen

Through It All

Words and Music by
Andraé Crouch

45

'Til the Storm Passes By

Words and Music by
Mosie Lister

When He Was On the Cross, I Was On His Mind

Words and Music by
Mike Payne and Ronny Hinson

The Blood Will Never Lose Its Power

Words and Music by
Andraé Crouch

He Is Here

Words and Music by
Kirk Talley

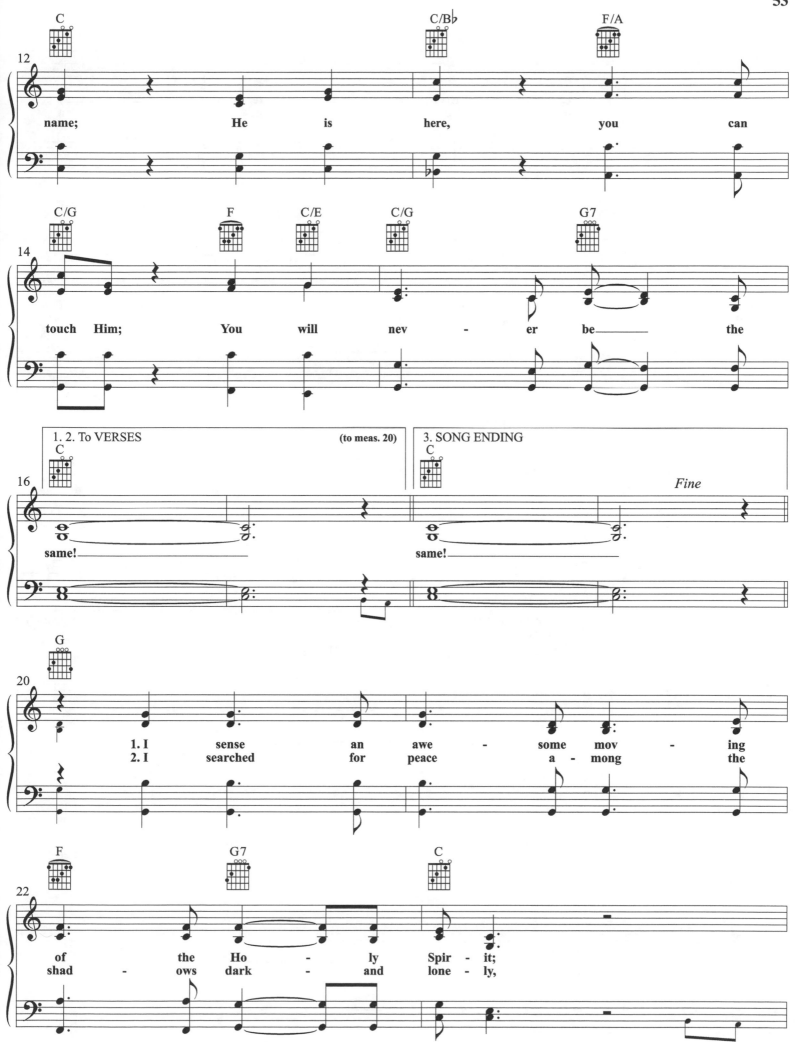

Holy Ground

Words and Music by
Geron Davis

Holy Is Thy Name

Words and Music by
Bill Stephen Henry

We've Come This Far by Faith

Words and Music by
Albert Goodson

Little Is Much When God Is In It

Mrs. F. W. Suffield and Dwight Brock

Mrs. F. W. Suffield

I Bowed on My Knees

Traditional

I Can't Even Walk
(Without You Holding My Hand)

Words and Music by
Colbert and Joyce Croft

I Just Steal Away and Pray

Words and Music by
Albert E. Brumley

It Won't Rain Always

Gloria Gaither

William J. Gaither and Aaron Wilburn

I've Come Too Far

Words and Music by
Nancy Harmon

There Is a River

Words and Music by
David Sapp

with pedal

There is a riv-er, ___ and it flows ___ from deep with - in. ___ There is a foun - tain ___ that frees the soul from sin. ___ Come to this wa - ter, ___ there ___ is a vast sup -

I Wish I Could Have Been There

Words and Music by
Wayne Haun and Joel Lindsey

1. Well a wom-an was healed when she touched the hem of His clothes;
2. He com-mand-ed Laz-'rus to walk right out of his grave,

That's just one of the sto-ries that ev-'ry-bod-y knows.
Gal-i-le-an storm He start-ed calm-in' the waves.

O, I wan-na

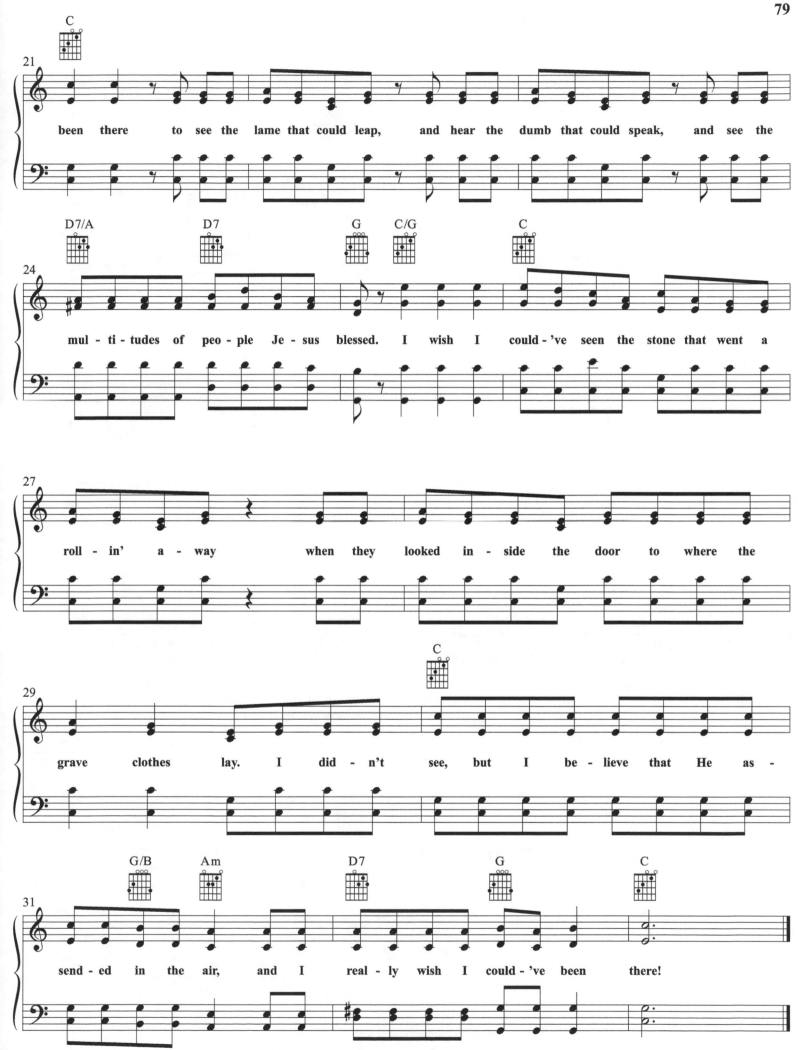

Champion of Love

Words and Music by
Phil and Carolyn Cross

The Love of God

Words and Music by
V. B. (Vep) Ellis

Oh, What a Savior

Words and Music by
Marvin P. Dalton

He Looked Beyond My Fault

Words and Music by
Dottie Rambo

Sweeter as the Days Go By

Words and Music by
Genser Smith

1. The more I trust Him, the more I love Him,
2. The mo-ment He saved me, His good grace He gave me, He

Noth-ing good for me He'll de-ny; The long-er I know Him, the
placed His love down deep in my heart; It's great joy in know-ing with

bet-ter I can show Him, I could-n't stop now if I tried.
Him I am go-ing, And nev-er-more from Him to de-part.

Oh, it gets sweet-er as the days go

The Night Before Easter

Words and Music by
Don Sumner & Dwayne Friend

The King Is Coming

William J. Gaither, Gloria Gaither
and Charles Millhuff

William J. Gaither

1. The— mar - ket place is emp - ty, No more traf - fic in the
2. Hap - py fac - es line the hall - ways, those whose lives have been re -
3. I can hear the char - iots rum - ble, I can see the march - ing

streets, All the build - ers' tools are si - lent, No more
deemed, Bro - ken homes that He has mend - ed, those from
throng, The— flur - ry of God's trum - pets Spells the

time to har - vest wheat; Bus - y house - wives cease their
pris - on He has freed; Lit - tle chil - dren and the
end of sin and wrong; Re - gal robes are now un -

la - bors, In the court room no de - bate, Work on
a - ged hand in hand stand all a - glow, Who were
fold - ing, Heav - en's grand - stands all in place, Heav - en's

What a Day That Will Be

Words and Music by
Jim Hill

The Lighthouse

Words and Music by
Ronnie Hinson

1. There's a light - house on the hill - side that
2. Ev - 'ry - bod - y that lives a - bout us says,

o - ver - looks life's sea, When I'm tossed it
tear that light - house down, The big ships don't sail this

sends out a light that I might see; And the
way an - y - more, there's no use of it stand - ing 'round; Then my

light that shines in dark - ness, now will safe - ly lead us o'er, If it
mind goes back to that storm - y night, when just in time I saw the light, Yes, the
Ah

Without Him

Words and Music by
Mylon R. LeFevre

O for a Thousand Tongues

Words and Music by
David Binion

Thanks

Words and Music by
Carroll McGruder

Who Am I?

Words and Music by
Rusty Goodman

1. When I think of how He came so far from Glo - ry,_____
2. When I'm re - mind - ed of His words, I'll leave thee nev - er,_____

— Came and dwelt true, a - mong the___ low - ly such as
Just be I'll give to___ you a life as for -

I,_____ To suf - fer shame and such dis -
ev - er,"_____ I won - der what I could have

grace, on Mount Cal - v'ry take my place,_____ It's then I
done to de - serve God's on - ly Son,_____ to fight my

He's Still Workin' on Me

Words and Music by
Joel Hemphill

God on the Mountain

Words and Music by
Tracy Dartt

Shout, Brother, Shout!

Words and Music by
Lari Goss

It's Still the Cross

Words and Music by
Niles Borop, Mike Harland,
Luke Garrett, and Buddy Mullins

With conviction (♩ = ca. 66)

1. It's not con - serv - a - tive or lib - er - al, how
2. We can wa - ter down the - ol - o - gy and preach a

ev - er they're de - fined; not a - bout in - ter - pre - ta - tion or the
word to suit our needs, we can jus - ti - fy sweet, sub - tle lies that are

judge - ments of the mind. It's the op - po - site of pol - i - tics,
wrapped in no - ble deeds. We can al - ter our con - vic - tions to a -

pow - er or pres - tige. It's a - bout a sim - ple mess - age, and
dapt to so - cial whims. But we can - not change the gos - pel, or the

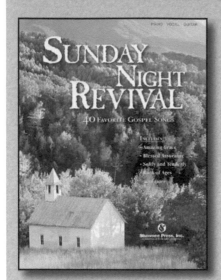
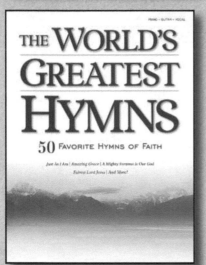
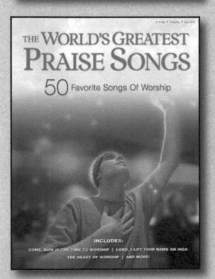
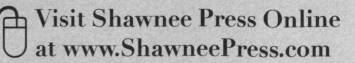